Rubbernecking

Rubbernecking

Poems by Molly Prosser

Word Poetry

Published by Word Poetry
P.O. Box 541106
Cincinnati, OH 45254-1106

ISBN: 9781625491671

Poetry Editor: Kevin Walzer
Business Editor: Lori Jareo

Visit us on the web at www.wordpoetrybooks.com

Acknowledgments

Grateful acknowledgement is given to the editors of the journals, collections, and magazines that first published the following poems, sometimes in earlier versions:

Blast Furnace ("Jogging," "Rubbernecking"); *Caesura* ("What's Left Behind"); *Carnival Magazine* ("Love Poem with Blackjack"); *Girls with Glasses* ("Four Letter Word, One Vowel," "Car Pooling"); *I-70 Review* ("Topography of a Body"); *La Fusta: Journal of Italian Literature and Culture* ("Devil Fish"); *Navigating the Heavens* ("Donation," "The Thickening Coat"); *Snakeskin Poetry Webzine* ("Good for You"); *So to Speak Journal* ("Metalwork," "Nesting"); *Soundings Review* ("Back in the Valley"); *Sugared Water* ("Dawn," "My Ex-Boyfriend's Ex-Drummer Used to Live in Texas"); *Utter Magazine* ("If Jesus Is the Key to Heaven, I'm Just a Girl in a Basement"); *VLP Magazine* ("From the Kitchen of...," "Resolutions from Liverpool"); *Voices in the Attic, Vol. XX* ("Port Macquarie, New South Wales," "What I Know about Being a Man"); *Weave Magazine* ("Almost," "The Battle at Breakfast").

My unending gratitude goes to Dr. Ellie Wymard, Jan Beatty, and the Carlow University MFA Program for their encouragement and support. A very special thanks to my spirit-guide and forever-mentor, Marion Winik, whose narrative skills and sage advice helped me shape this book. Inspiring me to be a better poet with her intense passion for writing, Michelle Stoner gets all of my admiration. Thank you to the universe for sending me my lifelong writing-retreat buddy and creative sounding board Elizabeth Smith. For their cheerleading and critiquing, cocktail-drinking and confidence-building, I give my thanks to Angela Bayout, Bethany Ruhe, Carla Raspanti Chichilla, Cindy Yogmas, and Heather Peters. Thanks to Joe DeFerrari for designing the most beautiful and haunting cover art. Much appreciation goes to my Bay Area writing family who keeps me creating, especially Laura Vrcek and Turi Fesler Steffen. And, thanks to my real family who gives me limitless stories to tell.

for Peter

Table of Contents

Museum of the Invention of Mankind

A Place Made for Leaving

My Mother Couldn't Prepare Me for This

Museum of the Invention of Mankind

"Life begins at the end of your comfort zone."
—*Neale Donald Walsch*

On a Date with Myself at the Monday $5 Movie

Everyone has a secret machine,
a quiet, internal technology
that sorts out the feminists from the porn stars,
that writes long, thin, ticker-tape lists,
that justifies the disappointment of bloodless bullfights,
that fasts and gorges and fasts when lovers are out of town,
that catalogs lyrics to Prince songs,
that gets library books back on time,
that craves meat out of windowless vans,
that creates panic at the thought of poisonous jellyfish,
that increases cheese intake,
that decreases the need for clean laundry,
that lowers voices to a whisper in the dark
just as the movie is about to begin.

Topography of a Body

If the truth of our childhood is hidden in our bodies, then mine lives in the tips of my fingers, burnt from canning tomatoes and salt-packing pickles,

or the insides of my nostrils singed by the cinnamon and clove and root beer extracts my mother poured into the bubbling sugar pots for hardtack,

or on my wrist where the scar still smiles up at me from when my father's quick slash at a venison roast caught my hand inside the carcass, holding back the entrails.

Hair the color of dishwater, skin the color of a cut raw potato, lips pink like boiled corned beef. I am a Sunday dinner, a ready feast, a fully-set table waiting for the bell.

Nesting

She thinks about the puffins hidden in the clutches of the black cliffs outside Reykjavik, huddled, alighting for haddock or herring as soft-spoken, thick-bearded men in their blinds cast nets

to catch them, trap them, midflight. They swallowed the chum from schooners, the plankton spewed from humpback feasts, gorging themselves until they were too fat to fly back to the volcanic shore and feed their hungry chicks.

She considers the killdeer faking a broken wing, protecting her nest from poachers, cooing and limping around her pile of rocks to distract her attackers, eggs rocking

slightly in the stones at the edge of the cracked parking lot. The raccoons are close, sick of dumpster scraps, craving the crack of speckled shells, the thick, golden yolk.

She opens her right hand, spreads her fingers apart and remembers how the Bantams' thin necks would fit in the spaces and how she would curl her hand around their soft, honey-colored heads,

her thumb stroking their beaks, the feathers between their eyes, calming them, loving them, getting them ready for the sharp twist of the wrist.

From the Kitchen of...

I used to watch my grandmother roll the dough across the counter,
bits of flour and butter pressed into the cracks of ceramic,
filling the gaps in the grouting. She told me no man would stay
unless I baked.

She liked to say goodnight to the apples and wedges of cheddar
before she tucked them in and made three quick incisions,
one for the Father, the Son, the Holy Ghost.

I'd have an Easter wedding, she decided. We'd bake the pies
in shifts, assembly-line style, wooden rollers clanking on the
countertops, crusts drying on makeshift racks, coils of apple peels
wilting in the garden.

Even now, in a diner in North Hollywood, I catch a whiff of warm
Macintosh and smoky cheese and think, I'll marry a man
with a black lunch bucket.

I'll cut him a slice of pie and wrap it in wax paper. He'll come home
late, maybe drunk, or maybe, if he follows his nose, on time.

Metalwork

I'm in my father's garage cutting siding for a hunting shanty
in a dead oil town in northern Pennsylvania. His voice is muffled
through the welding mask. He tells me to step back,
keep my eyes off the arc.

The weld pool, a mercury puddle just behind the tip of the heat,
makes a seam in the metal. I watch as the corrugated tin falls
in two pieces, slams on the concrete floor and topples the splintering
saw-horses.

It wasn't always about cutting. There were times he soldered.
His calloused hands melting the rungs of an iron ladder to a massive
iron frame, a homemade tree-stand that rested against a white birch
in the back yard. I would climb to the top, solid foothold after solid
foothold, and sit for hours staring at the
yawn of blue sky.

Now, waterfalls of light separate us. The ozone stench of the welding
circuit and chewing tobacco stains on the floor push us apart, keep us
at opposite sides of the metal until the inevitable break when we are
left alone, holding our halves.

What I Know about Being a Man

I kept bringing home rabid animals, feeding them when my mother
turned to hang the sheets on the clothesline, making leaf-dresses
for their weddings.

They said it had to stop, this constant concern for the frothing
groundhog, the baby fox that followed me
when I called it by name.

I was a pied-piper to the snarling dogs that tore apart our garbage
bags and pushed their snouts into the gut of my father's
hanging deer carcasses.

I loved each of them as long as I could with carrots and cabbage and
bits of corned beef. The day I was caught digging with a drooling
rabbit in the sandbox,

my father ended the game. Shovel in hand, blow after blow,
he kept hitting until I stopped crying.

The Polar Bears of Hershey Park

My older cousin Pat
showed me how to snake
my arm into the claw machine
at the Hershey Park arcade.
You make your hand skinny,
tuck your thumb into your palm,
and push it slowly past the plastic flap.

Fists full of synthetic fur, I fished
out stuffed polar bear after polar bear.
We shoved them down our shirts
and tried to play it "cool."

The story was that we'd won the bears,
that I found a five dollar bill in the park,
and Pat won them all for me. Everyone
told him he was so grown-up,
turning into a real man.

That night in bed, I kissed each bear
goodnight and listened to Pat make out
with his girlfriend on the porch. Through
the threadbare curtains, I watched him
tuck in his thumb and snake his
fingers up the back of her
Billy Idol tee shirt.

Simplicity #4272

smooth the vellum
transparent pattern
pinned to the
gingham silk.

trim the excess
fat until a fitted
dress is formed,
paintbrush-water blue
that hugs hips and
boosts tits
and twists up the
backline like licorice.

slip into the new machine,
the avalanche of fabric
with drifts of pleats
and piles of dime-store beads.

eat and drink and smoke all night
in a low-lit high school gym
where varsity wrestlers
(soon-to-be stock-boys)
all tug at the double-stitched seams.

If Jesus Is the Key to Heaven, I'm Just a Girl in a Basement

I think I was standing at the washing machine or was it the deep-freeze
doing delicates or maybe getting dad a pound of side-pork for breakfast
when Jesus our Lord and Savior smacked me on the back of my head
like a drunk great-uncle at a family reunion.

I've never had the dead stand so close behind me breathing and boxing
my ears, so I shrugged and said, *Okay, you obviously have something to say,
so shoot.*

To that, the Almighty said, *Shit, Molly, I'm on a tight schedule, so listen hard:*

> *Love makes life,*
> *hate makes death,*
> *and it's easy to re-claim swamp land if you have the right tools.*

I'd basically figured that out myself, so he left me there, feet getting cold
on the basement concrete, melting meat or fabric softener propped on my
hip, feeling pretty pissed off, since I didn't get to ask him what I wanted,
like should I get me some of that ole' time religion? And just where
can I find the Museum of the Invention of Mankind? And when will I
stop living like someone's looking? Living like I have a theme-song and a
laugh-track? And where do all the broken bits of hardware and silicone
and Swedish foam mattresses go when we stop needing them? And is
there a place where our mess is folded and molded into something new
like re-constituted tires turned into playground padding, a place where
hours of bedroom-eyed flirting with truckers becomes five blameless
twenties under the salt shaker and taillights on the highway?

There's a Problem in Japan

They've been hunting it for years to pickle/boil/fry,
but now the ships bob anchored among the humps
of flesh rotting in the harbors.

It was the food that bombs/embargoes couldn't stop,
a blubbery keystone that they're forgetting
with their pursestrings/tongues.

Now, the docks are bloodied with the husks of deflated
skin, the bays clogged with whaling hauls, spoils
of some war they can't stop fighting.

The Battle at Breakfast

Debbie stacks the toast and carefully cuts the pile into four
thin strips. No butter this morning – I want my soldiers sharp.
It's the first time I've waged war with a soft egg.

Debbie shows me how to decapitate the head, how to firmly
hold the egg cup and whack off the top of the shell, jam my knife into
the albumen and disrupt the yolk. Her thick Glasgow accent pours
over the carnage.

Slicing my way through the firm white with my first soldier,
I slowly probe the yellow center. I cut a path that others will follow.
The incision widens as one by one my burnt battalion gradually
descends to the center, absorbing the wreckage,
erasing the traces of battle.

Good for You

My sister and I would dare each other
at the dinner table, once we sucked the chicken
from the bone, to eat the white knuckle-joints.
There's a bump on the roof of my mouth
where I cut my gums trying to win.

The last to the marrow had to eat it.

Standing in line at 4am in the Hong Kong airport
waiting for a bowl of something you can't name, 37 hours
since your last meal, it's good to know true hunger. It's good
to let your body get so hungry that you remember
you're nothing special. You're nothing but a
break-it-down machine.

It's good to know the taste of bone so you can miss it.

What's Left Behind

In the Vietnamese noodle shop,
a one-armed man serves Pho
and chicken with lemongrass.
He balances the bowls
of steaming broth,
the platters of basil and
bean sprouts against his chest
and elbow and stump.

In bursts of broken English
he names the jars of condiments,
tells me to squeeze
slices of lime into my bowl,
stir and taste.
I force a smile, focus on his litany,
avoid his absent limb.

Through the steam of my soup,
I watch him wrap napkins
around chopsticks one-handed,
rolling them up into tight cocoons
on the sunflower tablecloths.

Jogging

There is nothing but the evil in and out
of January air, the rhythmic thud
of sneaker to sidewalk on a quiet Sunday,
the Pittsburgh grey sticking in my lungs
burning from bronchioli to brain

as a white cat with no ears
licks the tires of a white car
in someone's concrete driveway,

the hooves of aluminum reindeer
point to the sky, their mutilated half-bodies
resting behind the Sunoco station,

the Blockbuster Video manager,
a Tom Arnold look-alike,
the one who asked me once if I lived alone
and liked David Lynch,
empties the night drop box.

The Thickening Coat

The white cat is back
lingering in the garden,
reigning over the creeping
pumpkin vines and fallen acorns.

He's got feral thoughts and bloody
stains from grey squirrels, but seems
at ease inspecting the overturned earth,
breathing in the rotting summer peas.

Someone shaved him in choppy
swathes early this July when the heat
hung over the strengthening shoots
in our raised beds.

It was the same day Dottie
the decrepit beagle next door escaped
from her lead, intent on finding a slow,
secret, place.

But recently, I noticed the cat's thickening
coat, white fur slowly filling his flanks
again, assuring me that the cold will come,
reminding me of the oncoming drifts of snow.

Fourth River

I read my nightmare once on a stationary bike in a Kurt Vonnegut book
in a gym in the heart of Pittsburgh. I saw the faces of the Dresden men
sagging and wilted, the meat-hooks arched through their delicate throats,
their naked bodies hanging limp on tin walls, their uneven testicles
swaying slightly in the midsummer calm. I peddled faster, wondered
who else had seen my prophecy. Fifteen more miles, I told myself,
and I'd finally be thin.

I know there is a collective puddle, a pool we all use for our symbols,
but we like to think we're different. It's in the way someone else's alarm
sounds in the morning. Maybe Kurt dipped his toe in my section of the
swimming hole, and it worked for him, so he stole it. At sleepovers,
I used to wake up just before Erin's jazz-wolf alarm clock would start
to howl, and try to crawl over her to reach the red flower lapel button
and hit it before it could ruin my day with its snarling saxophone
wake-up song. And now, it's the way my heart pounds out of my throat
sharp as an ice pick when his alarm shocks the air with its inescapable
siren, and I jump awake hard and sweating in Detroit.

There's a river that runs beneath Pittsburgh, so I'm told. They have to
stop traffic and let it bleed now and then, at the intersection of Craig
and Fifth. It must be like the crook of an elbow there, a bend in the
underground flow where a pool forms and threatens to push up
manhole covers and street lamps. I used to go to the gym, but now I
run on these streets too poor to afford the air-conditioning, too soft to
stay at home, following the flow of the currents just under the sidewalk.
Kurt said we pick people to live out our happy fat with, and together
we move into our skinny days.

And that's the way it starts, *heavy*, sex all day and all night, kissing until
the skin peels off your lips, cheese and fancy crackers and Dijon mustards
and expensive fruits. But I know what's next. I've been that little girl
on the bicycle knocking on the doors of the bombed-out tenement houses
begging for my mother, watching old men play poker and smoke cigars
the color of the Monongahela after a pregnant rain. It's vaginal swelling.
It's bladder infections and thrush. It's cotton panties and cranberry juice
and yogurt and running is out of the question.

There are no signs for Toledo once you get to Toledo. I have a theory that this is true for all places. For every space, once you have arrived, there is no need to mention it. It is only in leaving that you call a spade a spade. The only way you can tell it's Toledo is the brick factory clinging to the edge of town, hanging over the riverbank, where piles and piles of rust-colored blocks line the highway, and all the signs tell you how to leave, how to get out, how to get to Dayton or Chicago or Canada or Detroit. I was on a steam train once when I was small, crossing the Kinzua Bridge two-hundred feet in the air,

the river a small garden snake from the window, when I began to faint. My father pushed my head between my legs, and my mother laughed, poked at my solid sides. I could just make out the folds of my crotch through my cotton jumper and smell the potato salad I spilled on my lap in the dining car and the sweat of that hot day.

Almost

I'm doing laundry to the soundtrack of *Bombay Dreams* on a smoky
corner of Liberty Avenue. My life is littered with mismatched socks,
saucerless cups, single chopsticks, pierogies in Little Italy, Bollywood
in Bloomfield. I shuffle a suitcase of dirty sheets down the street.

It used to be easy to predict the future by looking at the back of my
hand, reading the grid-work of blue pushing through my pale skin.
I remember the confidence of young fingers in the bed of an olive
El Camino at twilight creeping over the length of a boy.

The sloshing of the washing machine makes me smile, and I know
it's biological. I wonder what's inside a man, if I should fear it, what
I've released in the past. I read the confusion of freckles above my
wrist like drunken tealeaves at the bottom of a chipped China cup.

They all drown in my head, die suffocating and undignified deaths,
the men in the laundromat who watch me folding. They choke on
their 40s and no one comes to their funerals. They make me think of
buttons loosened by the wash, tethered by one limp thread.

A Place Made for Leaving

"Whenever you've exhausted setting, topic,
or tone, begin a new paragraph."
—*Lyn Hejinian,* My Life

Dawn

Three Dobermans crowd the sidewalk
massive haunches moving like barges,
slabs of meat beneath stretched skin.
A shepherd in pennyloafers yanks their leashes
bends their solid necks back when strangers pass.
Tethered together, they pull the morning light
across the city, open the matted, milky eye of day.
A man, palms smacking temples, eyes on the crumbling
curb approaches the pack, mumbling, twitching.
The beasts lunge, push him to the holly hedge,
their slippery teeth breaking the skin of his
elbows, his chin with each bark. They could
feel his hesitation, his aversion to the light,
his fear of beginnings.

Resolutions from Liverpool

This will be the year I learn to live alone.
I'll throw away plastic forks,
I'll use more paper towels,
I'll buy wine with the screw-tops.
The smell of grease will stop making me sick,
I'll eat chips and pasties and puddings
without considering the cholesterol.
I'll piss on dumpsters,
scream pornographic phrases at passing men.
I'll wear tank-tops non-stop.

I'll start the year climbing
up Hope Street in a sloppy snowfall.
I'll take a shortcut through the shell
of a bombed out church,
get a chip naan from a Punjabi nightclub,
take a shower in a bathroom that's not mine.
I've always been too prissy for my own good.

Wednesday at Shales

I'm just a little weary this happy hour watching the lawyers
and doctors hit on the withered bartender, her wrinkles cracking
the surface of her Mary Kay mask as she gives them gin and tonic
and rum and coke in styrofoam to-go cups with bendy-straws.

The brick-layers across the street chip at the facades of Fifth Avenue
storefronts getting the neighborhood ready for the white couples
to come with their park benches and Passats and Pomeranians,
invading the alleys of the Hill District. They're building apartments
for the fat girls in smart black dresses who work downtown, laugh
on their cell phones, give hand-jobs to their bosses, sit on my
barstool. The faces are getting whiter and whiter, and I'm seeing
ghosts in the bricks, shadows clinging to the sidewalks.

Fashion Never Takes a Day off

I met Vera Wang
at the bakery counter
of a San Fernando diner.

Her violet lips
turned up just a bit
like the collar of her Burberry blazer.

All I wanted were pancakes,
some sausage, or cornflakes,
but got some expert advice.

She told the girl behind me
that her belt was too shiny,
said I looked *uncomfortable* in black.

So, I stopped short and clocked her
in the middle of her A-line,
and she left with her lemon meringue.

Circus Liquor

I flip through the back issues of *People*
aimlessly, trying to decide on gin or a
six-pack. A twenty-foot neon clown winks
to life in the parking lot, illuminates the El
Chupacabra museum next door. Behind the Fritos
I glance at the chestnut-eyed cashier
as he rolls quarters and fingers his moustache.
He lifts his head – two plump Mexican girls
spill through the door: tube tops, acrylic
nails, knock-off purses. They brush past me,
grab armfuls of Dos Equis 40s and admire
themselves in the cooler condensation. Rubbing
her teeth with her index finger, the short one
asks, *Do I look like a chicana in these jeans?*

Consumption

In Vegas, the hookers have business cards with their pictures
and prices of tricks and hire bored Latina women to push them
on tourists as they leave the buffets. They snap the corners of the
cardstock, index finger to thumb, or slap the pack on the fat
of their palms to get men to look, to make eye contact.

Jet planes bisect the glittering Strip making incisions on the
monochrome sky, stitching the numbers of the cheapest hotels
and biggest black-jack tables. The skin on my forehead fissures
from the pollution, my fingers prune from the chlorine.

This is a shotgun town, and I want to get married for the free drinks.
If I'm not careful, I'll get everything I want. Our limo swerves to miss
the smackhead in the street, his pupils devouring his eyes, and that's
really the best we can do.

Tropicana Poolside

Three thin black boys
cut the surface of the water
jack-knife and laugh

A bedazzled sun hat
and three thick folds
from bikini top to bikini bottom

Grandfathers sleep on white towels
liverspots spread
over white knees and knuckles

11: 30 and he's drunk already
but this is Vegas, Nancy
his solid hide slaps the cement

From postcard to postcard
Grand Canyon, Memphis, Pittsburgh
she moves backwards across the country.

Back in the Valley

Brandy with an apricot gets dusty on a shelf in Rite Aid, Van Nuys,
California. I brush away the film, give it a good home. It's been four
years since I felt the skin of pollution. I remember where to buy the
best homemade salsa, the cheapest car-wash, El Pollo Loco.

This time, I'm a tourist. I say hello to the valley, Laurel Canyon
at dusk, watching from the overlook as San Fernando fights
off the night. It was always a fight in LA. Parking spots, wrinkles,
Scientologists.

Trying on a sunburn again, I remember the sin of tan lines.
I was always fine with pale skin, but this city can make anyone
insecure. Even cell phone towers look like palm trees or redwoods,
and only the layers of pavement keep the desert from moving.

On my lunch breaks, I used to watch the Armenian men gather
at Glendale Park to slam dominos on the concrete tables. I felt safe
listening to that solid sound.

Keeping House

Ilda moves baskets in the laundry room. Slides them across
the Moroccan tile. Royal blue and white. I can hear her over the
water. Boiling. We're working here

Ilda, the boxer-briefs, the bleach and me in the kitchen boiling
Ball jars. I move the bushel basket closer to the stove. Tomatillos.
The market was full of them today. Papery husks plumped with flesh

in my uncle's house, in this stucco palace. I'm just a boarder in the back
bedroom, but Ilda earns her keep. Charlie follows her cotton hem, tilts
his head in that idiot way. Pink slick tongue falls out.

He's like us – a guest between these walls. They found him in a
dumpster in the park. Eggshells and chicken bones. He still likes
small, dark spaces.

Boiling. The water splashes out of the canner off the jars out of the
pots of bobbing tomatillos. I pull at the stubborn skins. The emerald
cases. Ilda cleans her way through North Hollywood. Behind me,
I smell dirt and macaroons. Charlie, head tilted.

My uncle told me Ilda's husband killed her cousin in Ensenada
last year. Shot two kids and burned a house. I step back Ilda sweeps
where my feet were. She shoos the dog. I smile at her my fingers
burnt. Knuckles red hairless from the heat. Tomatillos ten to a quart
jar. They cook down to almost nothing but flavor.

Ilda watches me pack the jars. I think she's mad I'm here, mad I'm
home from work on a Tuesday. Making a mess. I promise I'll clean.
She stares opens the knife drawer

pulls out a long thin spatula. Slides the blade into my packed jars.
Tomatillos sigh. She moves the blade around the inside. I can hear
the air escape the bubbles disappear. I tilt my head.

Devil Fish

In a vendor's stall at La Bufadora, the devil fish clutch the wooden beams,
the stiff dead cartilage of the sting ray exposed, and I can't help thinking
that it's hard to hide the deep down, and soon we'll shed our feathery
bodies and everyone will see what's left, what's worth five pesos
and a cold Corona.

Walking from Venice

If the unicyclists and churro-sellers,
the hard-bodied muscle-men and
rainbows of glass marijuana pipes
and Virgin Mary conch-shell candles
become as ordinary as newspapers,
you can stop at the rows
of swing sets rising from the sand
just before the Santa Monica Pier.

It's worth one quick ride, back and forth,
watching the boardwalk disappear,
then re-appear, just beyond your flip-flops.

It will make you think of swinging
in your grandparents' backyard,
rocking the cheap tin poles in and out
of their postholes. You can almost feel
the thick hand on the small of your back,
making – then breaking – contact.

Climbing higher, pulling the chains harder
against your chest, it becomes easier to escape
the ground. You begin to feel safe at the top
of the arc, spiteful of the descent.

California will become cold, digestible.
A place made for leaving.

Car Pooling

Inching up the 101, we watch a fat rat climb the trunk of a long palm.
She's cooking a couple of kids in her gut. This night,
the breeze is cool off the desert.

We're eating exhaust and watching her bloated belly drag along the
palm bark. She looks like a hard-boiled egg
ready to crack.

She's struggling, concentrating as she pulls her fat load to the top of
the palm. She's got a nest up there, we guess, in the dead
fronds that refuse to fall.

I pull into the Diamond Lane, there are two of us on the way home
from the Strip, our jeep full of Hustler
porn and fast food.

The wind sifts through the open windows, and finally we're moving.
In the moonlight, I can just make out the yellow gleam
of her two pointed teeth.

I wonder if she had a car, an SUV, if she could drive the Diamond Lane.
She's got a pile of passengers inside of her, squirming. Surly,
the LAPD would let her be.

The pregnant, the split-personalities, the working dogs, the Siamese twins,
the haunted, the psychic – do they ride the Diamond Lane? Who's to say
when we're alone?

Enjoying My Own Company

I think I found it
last night on the floor
of my master bathroom,
the world sideways,
my fleshy cheek on the
toilet seat, a black bean burrito
swimming, regurgitated.
My Authentic Self smells
like processed corn.

I have rituals to get me through –
bubble baths, broken pills,
half a bottle of Australian wine.
If I'm lucky, that perfect pill
will close the day.

I touch my lamp three times,
close my drawers three times,
turn off the light three times
before I can fall asleep.
There's no one eagle-eyeing me,
so welcome home, Authentic Self,
the one my therapist embraces,
blurry from Tijuana pain killers.

Groggy, I think in terms of
theory and Mondays
in someone else's robe,
happy he's not here, but glad
I can smell his sweat on the terrycloth.

Alone, my Authentic Self eats more,
vomits more, types sappy letters
on a broken typewriter to my
grandmother (step-grandmother),
watches exercise videos sitting
on my couch re-writing lists
I wrote the day before.

My Ex-Boyfriend's Ex-Drummer Used to Live in Texas

above a fortune-cookie factory.
He told me that they fold them up
in those half-moons with big steam machines.
Thick, almond fog belches off the presses,
blows clouds of paper fortunes into the orange-lit
alley behind his apartment. In the morning,
the slips of paper would stick to his shoes.
He'd pull them off on the bus, one by one,
soggy visions of what could be.

Secretarial Work

I'm taking notes shorthand on leadership and strategic
planning for a group of Russian teachers. The women
talk of liberation and representation, my ink puddles,

and I catch myself staring at the back of a Siberian siren
as she leaves quietly for the bathroom. I wonder what
the toilets are like in Russia, wonder if they're like
the ones in England with the water so far from the seat

that when you pee it echoes and never splashes back.
There's more talk of financial stability, of organizational
policy, of workforce potential. I worry that this is my one skill.

The thin Oksana taps her pen on the conference room table,
and I'd like to take her for a drink, tell her not all Americans
are volunteers. We're not all smiles and sunshine. Tell her, I've
had sex on this table after work when my bosses went home,

I'm not just a minute-taking drone, but the meeting ends with
business cards and handshakes, and I'm left to wash the teacups
and push in the chairs.

Port Macquarie, New South Wales

The heat moved into our room
on violent birdsong
and nightmares.

I rose naked to pull the blinds
turn on the fan
and got caught in the
cacophony of screaming parrots.

It was like underwater techno
electronic nuances
only machines could produce.

Staring at the strangler figs
outside our window
I listened to your shallow breathing
the terrifying warbles
the new murmur of night.

Cabin Pressure

Sometimes, the constant ticking of my biological clock stops,
the hands freeze and stick on an arbitrary time, say, 2:49am
on a flight from Dublin with a long, drawn-out descent
into JFK, when pressure pushes on the tiny eardrums
of sleeping babies and suddenly, I'm surrounded
by shrieking, and I can see their mothers,
powerless, dreaming of Manhattan
bathed in mid-morning light.

Girl Missing White

Just before the Hotel Yorba, that grey monster with the red block
Hollywood-style letters Y-O-R-B-A propped by a scaffolding
skeleton, there was an amber alert on the construction signs. They
flashed *Caution*   then   *Slow Down, Save a Life*,   then   *Girl*

Missing

White

1993 Mercury   Call 911. The sky was amber with Daylight Saving's
newness as I fled Detroit with another UTI or maybe it was
break-through bleeding. I always wondered the day after if
pregnancy hurt, not the having

but the getting. Did getting pregnant hurt, and not the actual screwing,
but the moment that sperm found egg, did that hurt? On overpasses,
bridges to Canada, amber, Ann Arbor, amber, this girl was
really missing

out on this sky. It was April just before it got warm, but the light
fooled you out of your sweater and the sun tricked the crocuses and
everyone had their windows rolled down in the Motor City even though
it was far too cold. She was stuffed in a white car like a pimento
in an olive

swimming in the dirty martinis I drank the night before. I'd like to warn
her about what boys can do, about bladder infections. I had to pull over
at the first rest stop outside of the city, and almost fell off the seat for the
burning. I knew my doctor would ask, so I stood up to look
in the bowl, the blood

a telltale sign I screwed up. If I were bad, my mom used to make me
sponsor these poor little girls from somewhere in South America or Africa
with my allowance. I had one once who knew

my name and colored me a picture. It was a tree, the leaves were red,
burnt orange and cracked brown, but if I'm being honest it really wasn't
that good, and the only reason I kept it

was guilt. Maybe if she were better at drawing trees, maybe if she weren't
my punishment, I'd be willing to remember her, or the amber alert,
or the   *White*   *1993 Mercury*

Girl   Missing   White   Girl   Missing scrolling across I-75, but all I can
really think about are my burning insides.

Love Poem with Blackjack

I'm standing at a carving station
in the downtown Detroit casino
listening to a Motown cover band
in sequined lycra belt *R-E-S-P-E-C-T*,
as the stench of warm meat
seeps into my jean jacket.

I'm just waiting for you
to get done with the blackjack
so we can cruise Greektown,
find a little dive with plastic olive vines
and checkerboard tablecloths,
get high in the alley before the appetizer
and laugh at the flaming cheese.

I placed a bet on a roulette wheel
earlier tonight just to hear
the tickety-tack,
but you know I always lose
like the liverspotted ladies
in sweat-pants who push in quarters
and rub their rosary beads
for a line of sevens.

Just behind the kosher franks
past the penny slots and keno tables,
I see your fingers pull at the air
calling *hit me*
and I want to tell you that this is America,
you might just get lucky.

My Mother Couldn't Prepare Me for This

"Never go with a hippie to a second location."
— *Alec Baldwin,* 30 Rock

Rubbernecking

In the sterile moment just before the explosion, we watch a doe
on the side of the freeway pull her hoof from the crosswork
of a grocery cart and hobble up the exit ramp. It's not yet dawn,
but I'm thinking

about the derrick in my parent's front yard, the mechanical rhythm
of learned sex. I've sacrificed to power grids, worshiped at the edge
of chemical reservoirs, kept the gentle hills and short thick forests
from invading

my blood. On this cold highway, the day pinking up like a
transplanted lung, we wait for the ripple of smoke and glass
to blanket us, the bulwark of artificial heat from the tractor-trailer
fire to kiss our foreheads, the shower of burning corn-chip bags
to litter the burm, crackling as the fat and foil disappear

into cinders. We can't stop watching the gruesome trainwreck
of a truckwreck, breathing the burning of wanderlust. Locomotives
were romance once, railroads punctuating canyons and rimrock
like perpetual courtship, womanhood rising dangerously to meet
our pioneer vision, and I want to prove

I can leave.

In the Exact Middle of the Night
after Susan Stewart

He's talking taxes in his sleep, his arms wrapped around my chest
tight as tinfoil grinding his teeth on the back of my neck, and I'm
absentmindedly worrying

about my car, the shocks are bad, and it won't pass inspection, and
his grip gets tighter, like he doesn't want to admit I could leave
when he dozes off,

drive into the Detroit night, but I'm glad his worries are on the back
of my neck, grinding. I did my taxes already and got my refund,
used it to get my locks changed

after the break-in when the crack-whores from next door rifled
through the basement, and I'm lying here thinking about the
K9 dog that tore down the front door after them,

and I want to buy a house, I want a house with him, but I've got
secrets to replace secrets, and I guess I was supposed to feel safe
as I watched the dog's face contort

as it snarled at the German words, its badge gleaming on its bullet-
proof dog-vest, but didn't, not until tonight, not until he told me
with his teeth

that we'll keep finding a center, and at the center of everything
is another center.

Flower Show

We say our goodbyes in the warmth of the stairway
as the lace of frost retreats from my windshield.
It's early in Michigan. The tractor trailers
on the turnpike rumble past me,
eating at the cold silence.

In my headlights, I can see each snowflake.
Some are wild, white orchids exploding
as they hit the glass, foreign and exotic.
Others are tulips, pale, lingering
long enough for me to make out their
heart-shaped petals.

Beneath the glassy mirror of snow fields
along the freeway, I catch glimpses
of the waking city. On these dead mornings,
only spring waits.

Penelope on My Sleeve
for Margaret Atwood

My city is lonely when you go,
   and you say yours is, too,
     but no man will ever kill himself
      for the love of me.

Yet you insist on the visits, and which of us,
   really, can resist the temptation
     of being indispensable?

You think you're tricking me into coming
   or staying longer than I should,
     so I let you tell the stories that will define us,
      weaving threads I can't unravel.

I've heard about your fatherless days, and know
   you want to set something loose in this world –
     a legacy, perhaps, to swell up my belly,
      a force that can be set into motion.

Unification

I thought once, at a Gang of Four concert, that I should have sex
with an older man. An *old* man. A man older than my age doubled
who grew grey facial hair. A man who could tell me history from an
informed perspective. On stage, the band broke microwaves and
freezers with baseball bats. Their muscles looked tight in the floodlights.
Old men pounding appliances. It would be like an erotic time-travel,
years wrapping around me like legs. My body absorbing the past.

Months later, just south of the Mason Dixon line, I decided
I was wrong. A young man with a soft face convinced me to pull over.
He wanted to straddle the divide, one foot Union, one Confederate.
He thought it would be funny. We picked our way through the dead
leaves, the flapping screen door of the ramshackle Mason Dixon Motel.
He saw it first, a pheasant rotting in the autumn air, pulled me from
the corpse. He drove the rest of the way home. In the failing light,
he asked me about the war. About Gettysburg. Lincoln. He cringed
when I told him the rivers ran red. We talked about the histories
we learned. Or heard. Or read somewhere.

It's Not So Fragile

I try on your extra bathrobe
   wear it to the breakfast table
   while you fry eggs hard and tomatoes,
   bring me coffee.

I push my cold feet into the crook
   of your knee
   while Michigan snow piles on the balcony,
   and you hold my toes until the blood comes back.

I rearrange your dresser drawers
   socks on the left
   put your dishes where I think they should be,
   and you kiss my forehead for cleaning.

I talk too much to strangers
   who steal your seat and touch
   my leg when you leave to smoke,
   but you come back and buy us all another round.

Record-Breaking

We're doing the hucklebuck up
the switchbacks just outside Sedona
trying to decide the correct spelling of color –
O-R or O-U-R.

He hates being wrong
so he knows the price of hotels
like the Beverly Hills, the bungalow suites,
takes pictures of signs to remember
how many miles to Big Sur,

tells me this morning England
was the hottest it's ever been.

We talk names for babies
we've not yet conceived
make sure they're bully-proof
and tease-tested,
play word games to pass the time
on the freeway to Phoenix,
our six-month anniversary in the bag.

He asks my thoughts on eco-living
as we ring hollow bells at Cosanti,
the showcase *City of the Future*,
smoke cigarettes in a clay workshop,
snap pictures of the saguaro cacti
that line the gravel parking lot.

We're on the Sonny Bono
towards Palm Springs,
wind farms flanking us
working like giant pinwheels
when we see the Mustang flip.
Breathless, I slam on the brakes.

He's sure no one survived.
I rest my hand on his knee,
stroke his leg until he relaxes
and the color –
or colour –
comes back to his face.

Donation

There's a strange starvation between times
that brings me back to the chair,
opens my thick vein,
makes me bleed on my lunch-hour.

It feels wrong, dangerous to like the burn
in the crook of my arm, the delicate
tethering of flesh to steel to silicone,
the hot pain of stretched surgical tape on skin.

I saw a girl once who bled so fast
the tubes burst, and none of the nurses noticed.
She lay there sighing, reading the newspaper.
I watched her drain out.

The nurse smacks my leg and smiles,
lets me know I'm finished. She places the bag
of hot blood on my thigh and I wonder
how many more pints until I reduce to nothing

but warmth.

They Could Have Told Me

that Vancouver held my future in her hands
three months before I arrived, that we slept in the same hostel
in Gastown, bought muffins from the same organic coffee shop.

The totems say there is only one raven, one evergreen,
one thick-bellied orca, but forgot to mention that two of us
sat on the same bench in Stanley Park in the same moody rain,
told the same one-eyed bum to stop following us.

We separated, not knowing each other, empty like the abalone
shells in the tall grass behind English Bay, while the totem poles
fixed their gazes skyward enjoying the show.

A Four-Letter Word, One Vowel

He's got on his dressing-gown swagger, all confidence and mid-
morning piss and vinegar. He marches down the hard-wooded
hallway, sits beside me at the breakfast table for the morning
crossword. His genitals rest on the unfinished pine chairs.
They look natural there, like part of the kitchen. He doesn't look
funny naked, smoking his cigarette.

When I was younger, my mother showed me a *Playgirl*. She didn't
want me to be surprised by the real thing. The men in the magazine
had their penises draped over things – armchairs, windshields,
tree stumps. One was holding a briefcase and a pile of manila
folders. Their expressions were quite grave, and I couldn't
understand what was so serious. They looked insane with their
privates out, willy-nilly.

In his wide-open robe, he's contemplating the capital of Peru and the
ruling dynasty of China during the construction of the Great Wall.
It's all very serious. His eyes drill into me as he asks about Mozart's
final opera. My mother couldn't prepare me for this.

Badwater

We talk about going lower, the Dead Sea, maybe, when Israel
gets itself sorted or getting hotter in Libya but this is pretty hot and
as low as you can go in this country so we race from air conditioned
car to vista to car to vista

and every time we open the door it reminds me of Thanksgiving,
that blast of heat from the oven when my mother makes me check
the turkey and potatoes or when David my beautician puts me under
the hair dryer and it feels like fire on my neck

and I can't stop taking pictures of the plants, impressed that they live
here in Death Valley that anything lives near Furnace Creek, the
sagebrush and dead stalks at Devil's Cornfield, the plump yellow
bladder pods and desert parsley, and he keeps telling me

to look up, look out at this, the painted rocks at Artist's Palette
and our bananas rot in the cooler as we stare at the iron ore blue
waterfalls and pink decaying seashells,

the white so bright our camera won't work, so we put it in the glove
box to cool, and neither of us notice the gas light and it's 17 miles
to the nearest station and this is a hire car,

how many gallons do you think we have, really, or should we just
call AAA, wait at a casino and play Texas Hold'em until the tow-
truck comes to drag us, ashamed, away from the valley,

like it beat us, like some bully who stole our milk money, but we're
both too proud for that, so we push on, secretly calculating
how many miles we could walk in this heat,

remembering what the Park Ranger said at Lone Pine, not to move
if we got stuck, stand still in the car shadow, *the heat will kill you*, and
I'm white-knuckling the steering wheel

when some Western larkspur catches my eye, a purple flash,
and I think we'll make it to the Cherry Patch, we can see the pink
sign, voted "Best Little Whore House in Nevada" by the local VFW,

and the gas is cheap and I buy red licorice and water and a map
to Las Vegas with all the brothels and porn shops
marked with red printed kisses.

Old Farmers Don't Know

They say this was an ordinary winter
true to the almanac,

> but people went bankrupt on 8th Avenue
> and married a junkie with a ruby ring
> and switched to soy milk
> and bought two cats and started to knit
> and let a steelworker into their bed
> and got hate mail from Ann Coulter
> and told their boyfriend it was a miscarriage
> and learned to mambo
> and watched koalas sleep over Sausage Gully
> and whales die in Prince Albert Sound
> and moved to Scottsdale in a stolen Escort
> and fed wild green parrots out of their hand
> after an ice cold shower.

They say the sun rose and set
like clockwork.

House Hunting in Cheshire

We're looking for houses in newspapers, websites. Online realty
offices. Page after page of duplexes, semi-detached bungalows,
cottages. I can't find the basements. He says I'm a basement
kind of girl, dying for brick-wall security.

I tell him that it's good to know there's something below
your feet instead of hanging over your head. He likes lofts.
Attics with wooden beams. He feels better with it all suspended
above him. He likes looking up.

There are no basements in England. Concrete slabs under
floorboards. I wonder where I'll keep my canning jars. Where
will our daughters play spin-the-bottle, our sons
hide their dirty magazines?

It's an American thing, basements, our realtor points out. She shows
us lofts. Pull-down staircases. Insulation pads and peaked roofs
and octagon windows in the apex. I say, *show us a cellar.*
She distracts me with gardens.

Patchwork patios and pebble fountains. Brick walls, ivy, hedgerows,
and alleyways. *Just think of them as basements without ceilings,*
she says. I walk step-stone to step-stone. The sky buckles
under the weight of grey.

Upon Opening an Invitation to My 10-year High School Reunion

Just like that
it happens in scary movies
when the hero has a scary
dream the kind of dream
where legs move like barges
and the killer tomatoes are chomping
at the back door pounding, evil catsup
dripping from their fangs
and then *POOF* we realize
it was all just a dream a scary
nightmare and the sexy lead
wakes with a start that sits him bolt
upright sweaty in his bed all tangled
up in damp sheets panting   panting
panting   calming down   and he leans back
on his elbows satisfied that there are no
such things as monsters and no one is under
the bed in the closet behind the bedroom door
that the really REALLY bad thing happens
cause the quiet brings it on the quiet like in
dreams but this is a deep quiet a *real* quiet
and monsters can live between the gasps for air
right in the heavy pauses in heavy breathing
and then there's *real* running and *real* high-heel
breaking, and *real* falling on broken branches and
real chainsaws and *real* voodoo and *real* flesh-eating
monkeys and really fucked up Freddy Krueger shit
that will keep you up for days not sleeping
not blinking and certainly not dreaming.

Because I've Outsmarted Biology

I'd have a baby for the perks. I'd have a big fat baby so I can park
closer to Trader Joe's like the handicapped, board planes early,
make people move for me on the bus. I'd eat cocktail sausages
and pickled cauliflower, scoop peanut butter out of the tub
with a Snickers bar. I'd have an excuse to stay in.

My plump baby will wail and howl when I'm in line at the bank,
reminding everyone just how shit waiting in line at the bank is.
I'd take my baby to a fancy play and let it chest-cough all the way
through Macbeth, or maybe spit-up oatmeal at the opera.

And in the twilight fog of an interstate rest-stop, I'd pull my baby
out of his seat, groggy and blinking, his eyes clamped shut as I fix
his hair, his jumper, tie his shoes. I'd take his outstretched hand
and silently lead him inside. He'd follow me anywhere.

He'd have to.

Bedtime Story

It's sappy like a Hallmark card or a slow-dance song, but there are a
million colors of dawn and dusk and I want to see them all with you
in the back of a Volkswagen bus.

I got nowhere stuck in a Hilton in Cleveland watching *Murder, She Wrote*
and documentaries on wild horses, waiting for other people to sort out
the helix of our bones, so I ordered Chinese food for three and thought
about how I needed to meet a man like you.

The land of Room Enough and Time Enough isn't enough for me –
I want every place imprinted with our movements, I want to trick
a Venn Diagram, and land is just a character in our morality play,
a piece of flesh to be devoured, a John Ford drama.

I know to be American is to be male, the breezy openness of it all,
but they tell women a secret when we're born here, they whisper it
while we sleep – only the rocks are real, and they callous our hearts
until the veins are black knots we can never untangle.

I'll show you what you need to know about this place. It's so many
things you can't see. It's romance in the West, it's men who kill horses
and eat the insides of clocks to keep the time from passing,
it's a lot like drowning.

It's over-medication, a Puritan work-ethic and private compulsions,
it's travel that makes you conscious of borders. It's half-hidden
in the thunderstorm of a New Mexico night, half in the smile
of a boy selling sticks of Doublemint at an underpass, and
everything's up for discussion.

We've met the angel of departure, and since there's no proof that this
is a fairy tale, it must be true. This country is the big open brunt of it,
cottonwood trees swallowing up the rivers, corn fields disappearing
under the weight of the stars, strip malls and car dealerships our
enchanted forests, our junkyards of love.

A Last Look Around

Street lamps ease awake to meet the oncoming black. It's late August,
and night takes its time, sits down slowly on Pittsburgh.

Hospitals open and libraries close, inhaling and exhaling bodies to the
street in blasts of air conditioned cool. I'll miss this city when I'm gone –

the way the sirens sound a long escalating whine, the way the traffic hums
just a bit lower than in England, the way lemons and artichokes are cheap.

Hibernating, I wait until spring when things start over, and a year of lean
can put on weight. These three rivers will swell and swallow their wharfs,

but I'll be surrounded by ocean. We'll have his mother to watch the dogs
or babies, his sisters to tell me where to buy tampons.

The fall will come with no Thanksgiving, no Polish festivals or pumpkins,
and I'll find myself longing for dead leaves and banks of dirty snow.

Biographical Note

Molly Prosser is a freelance Editor and Content Strategist for e-retailers and internet start-ups. She holds a BA in English from Penn State and an MFA in Creative Writing from Carlow University where she has taught Literature, Marketing Writing, and Communication. Although she's a Pittsburgher at heart, Molly currently lives in Oakland, CA with her husband and mini dachshund.

❦ ❦ ❦ ❦

Made in the USA
Charleston, SC
11 March 2016